AMTP Pedagogy Course Study Guide

George Graham, PhD
Virginia Tech
Blacksburg, Virginia

Human Kinetics Publishers

ISBN: 0-87322-407-8

AMTP Director: Scott Wikgren
Acquisitions Editor: Linda Anne Bump, PhD
Managing Editor: Julia Anderson
Assistant Editor: Dawn Roselund
Copyeditor: Merv Hendricks
Proofreader: Karin Leszczynski
Production Director: Ernie Noa
Typesetter: Ruby Zimmerman
Text and Cover Design: Keith Blomberg
Text Layout: Denise Lowry
Illustrations: Dick Flood and Kathy Boudreau-Fuoss
Cover Image Based on Photo by: Bob Veltri
Printed by: Versa Press

Printed in the United States of America

10 9 8 7 6 5 4 3 2 1

Human Kinetics Publishers
Box 5076, Champaign, IL 61825-5076
1-800-747-4457

Canada Office:
Human Kinetics Publishers
P.O. Box 2503, Windsor, ON N8Y 4S2
1-800-465-7301 (in Canada only)

Europe Office:
Human Kinetics Publishers (Europe) Ltd.
P.O. Box IW14
Leeds LS16 6TR
England
0532-781708

Australia Office:
Human Kinetics Publishers
P.O. Box 80
Kingswood 5062
South Australia
374-0433

Contents

Introduction

The *AMTP Pedagogy Course Study Guide* is a chapter-by-chapter companion to the textbook *Teaching Children's Physical Education: Becoming a Master Teacher*. This study guide is designed to help you gain maximum benefit from the text as well as the AMTP Pedagogy Course and the Self-Study Video. It will also help you prepare for the AMTP Pedagogy Course take-home test. In addition, the study guide offers you opportunities to reflect on your own teaching and philosophies.

As you are completing the study guide, keep in mind that its purpose is to prompt meaningful interaction with the course content. Think about the questions and exercises as they relate to your teaching environment or situations you have experienced as a student. I'm confident that by successfully completing the Pedagogy Course, you'll heighten your effectiveness as a children's physical educator.

STUDY GUIDE INSTRUCTIONS

You'll complete some of the exercises in the study guide during the Pedagogy Course. The other questions and exercises you will complete independently. Before attempting to do any of the take-home questions or exercises, read *Teaching Children Physical Education: Becoming a Master Teacher* thoroughly. As you read, consider how you can apply the information to your current or future situation.

Once you've read *Teaching Children Physical Education*, you are ready to complete the study guide. At the beginning of each chapter, objectives are listed. Read the list of objectives, and if they are not familiar, review the chapter in the text. Once you understand the objectives, you are ready to complete the questions and exercises. If you feel you can't answer a question, reread the corresponding section of the text.

If problems arise, if anything is unclear, or if you have any questions, contact the AMTP National Center at 1-800-747-4457. A staff member will be happy to help you.

AFTER COMPLETING THE STUDY GUIDE

After completing the study guide, you are ready to take the Pedagogy Course take-home test. You are free to use the text, the study guide, and the self-study video as references in doing the test. Return your test for grading to AMTP within 3 months after the course is completed. A score of 90% or better is required to pass the test. Anyone scoring lower than 90% will be invited to retake the test. (You can retake it as many times as necessary.)

When you have successfully completed the test, you will be awarded an AMTP Pedagogy certificate of course completion.

BECOMING A MASTER TEACHER

Successful completion of the Pedagogy Course is a step toward earning recognition as a Master Teacher through AMTP. If you haven't taken the AMTP Content Course, that is your next step. Information on course dates and sites is available from the AMTP National Center.

If you have already successfully completed both the Pedagogy and Content Courses, you may apply for entry into the Master Teacher Practicum. For application information, again contact the AMTP National Center.

FOR MORE INFORMATION

Excellent elementary physical educators are always trying to learn more. For more information on the full line of elementary physical education resources and programs available from Human Kinetics Publishers, contact

Child Health Division
Human Kinetics Publishers
Box 5076
Champaign, IL 61825-5076
(1-800-747-4457)

Chapter 1

Successful Teaching

Objectives
As a result of completing the tasks in this chapter you will be able to

- develop a deeper understanding of the personal experiences that influence your views of successfully teaching children's physical education;
- identify factors related to teaching children physical education that are personally satisfying or are perceived as challenges or obstacles; and
- understand your personal goals for your program of physical education for children.

THE TEACHER, NOT ONLY THE CONTENT

The first chapter in *Teaching Children Physical Education* begins with a quote by Woody Allen that reveals a lack of respect for physical education teachers. Briefly describe five experiences that Allen might have had that contributed to his loss of respect for P.E. teachers.

1.

2.

3.

4.

5.

In groups of three or four, compare your situations with others in the class. Are any the same? What does that tell us about how physical education may have been taught in the past?

ANALOGIES OF TEACHING

Imagine yourself teaching children in a gym or on a playground. Describe exactly what is happening: What content are you teaching? Where are you standing? Are you talking? If so, to whom? Think of two more teaching scenarios and briefly, but specifically, describe them.

Scenario 1:

Scenario 2:

Scenario 3:

In chapter 1 I present three analogies of teaching—some compare teaching to being in the eye of a hurricane, others to being the ringmaster in a circus or the conductor of a symphony orchestra. For each of the three scenarios you described, indicate which analogy best matches your feelings about yourself in that particular scenario. Compare scenarios and analogies with someone else. What factors do you think might influence your choice of analogies: Your previous teaching experience? The context of the school? The content being taught? The grade level of the children? What does this tell you about yourself as a teacher?

CHANGING AND DYNAMIC

Teaching children's physical education is an occupation that is constantly changing and dynamic—not static and predictable. Do you consider change an advantage or disadvantage? Working alone or with a partner, describe three advantages and three disadvantages of working in a constantly changing situation.

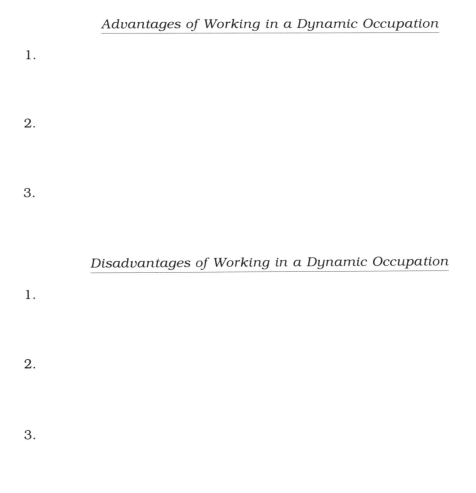

Advantages of Working in a Dynamic Occupation

1.

2.

3.

Disadvantages of Working in a Dynamic Occupation

1.

2.

3.

Reflect on your personal work preferences and lifestyle. Do advantages outweigh disadvantages? Or do you prefer a more predictable work setting? What, if any, implications does this have for how you might teach?

THE CHALLENGE OF TEACHING CHILDREN'S PHYSICAL EDUCATION

Throughout *Teaching Children Physical Education*, I tried to portray teaching in realistic settings. In the first chapter, I list benefits and obstacles related to teaching children physical education. Make a list of the top five benefits and the five most difficult challenges for you as a P.E. teacher. Try to list challenges and benefits not included in the chapter.

Challenges (from most to least challenging)

1.

2.

3.

4.

5.

Benefits (from most to least beneficial)

1.

2.

3.

4.

5.

When you complete your list, discuss the benefits and obstacles in small groups. What do your two lists reveal about your current or future satisfaction as a P.E. teacher?

PERSONAL DEFINITION OF "SUCCESSFUL"

In the first chapter *successful* is defined, in part, as children developing positive attitudes and teachers feeling satisfied with their jobs. Dream for a few minutes about what you want your students to learn, know, and feel about physical education. What would you like to have accomplished with your students when they leave your program after 5 or 6 years? Figure 1.2 (pp. 8-9 of the text) may be helpful to you as you dream about your teaching goals. Now, in words someone not in physical education could understand, write down your specific responses to these phrases:

As a result of being in my P.E. program for several years, I would like my students to *learn:*

As a result of being in my program for several years, I would like my students to *know:*

As a result of being in my program for several years, I would like my students to *feel:*

Chapter 2

Planning to Maximize Learning

Objectives
As a result of completing the tasks in this chapter you will be able to

- develop a keener understanding of your tendencies and beliefs regarding planning;
- develop the ability to analyze available instructional time and understand implications for planning; and
- compare and analyze planning differences for beginning and experienced teachers.

YOUR PERSONAL PLANNING STYLE

Teachers have various planning styles. Some teachers prefer to plan early in the morning before school; others write their plans before they leave school at the end of the day; some plan in the evenings. Others use the commute home as planning time. Specifically describe the time, setting, and environment in which you plan. Do you prefer it to be quiet? Or do you prefer music or the television on as you plan?

My Planning Environment:

Compare your planning preferences with others. How important is it to have a planning environment that is desirable for you? Why?

CALCULATING INSTRUCTIONAL TIME

Using Tables 2.1 through 2.3 in the text as reference, determine the actual number of minutes you would have as a teacher if you taught physical education once a week to a class of kindergarten children. (Refer to the figure on page 14 also.) How many minutes would this allow you to spend on each instructional objective for kindergarten for that year?

Kindergarten

Actual number of minutes _____

Number of minutes per objective _____

Now assume you are teaching fifth graders who have physical education three times a week. According to Kelly (Tables 2.1 to 2.3), how much actual learning time would the children have—and how many minutes would this allow for each objective?

Fifth Grade

Actual number of minutes _____

Number of minutes per objective _____

What do these figures tell you about the time children have in P.E. classes? Refer to Tables 2.1 through 2.3 and describe how a teacher might gain more instructional time. Be specific and realistic. Few teachers, for example, get to decide how many days per week students will attend P.E. class.

LEARNABLE PIECES

Chapter 2 of the text asks you to estimate how long it will take children to learn various skills and behaviors. Write your estimates below.

Skill, Concept, or Behavior   *Estimated Time to Learn*

Second graders to learn
difference between sym-
metrical and asymmetrical
shapes

Third graders to catch a
gently thrown ball from a
distance of 50 feet

Fifth graders to cooperate
when working in groups

Now select a skill you know well, such as throwing, kicking, or jumping and landing. Identify several cues or critical components that characterize an efficient performance of that skill. How many minutes will it take children to learn that cue so that it becomes automatic without having to concentrate? There is no right answer, but it is interesting to compare perceptions. List cues and time estimates.

Skill (Cues)   *Estimated Time to Learn*

1.

2.

3.

Try to compare and discuss your answers with others. What implications do your responses have for how you plan your lessons?

BEGINNING AND EXPERIENCED TEACHERS' PLANNING

Figures 2.1 and 2.2 in the text show how experienced and beginning teachers plan a class. Assume that you observed both teachers teach and that both were good. Why would a beginning teacher's plan be longer? Do you think the experienced teacher was being lazy?

In a group, discuss the information that the experienced teacher may have stored away that allows him or her to write a briefer plan than the novice teacher.

THE TENDENCY TO AVOID PLANNING

Most teachers agree planning is an important prerequisite to a successful physical education program. Yet some tend to plan minimally, or not at all, for classes and simply rely on a "bunch of fun games" or a "bag of tricks" rather than developing a learning program. List five reasons it is important to plan and then list five reasons some teachers tend to avoid planning. Complete this section by reflecting on your own planning tendencies and beliefs.

It Is Important to Plan Because

1.

2.

3.

4.

5.

Some Teachers Tend to Avoid Planning Because

1.

2.

3.

4.

5.

Method for calculating amount of available instructional time and the number of objectives that can be addressed

A = # of weeks of school per year:

B = # days of instruction per week:

C = Length of instructional period in minutes:

D = Instructional time available per year (A × B × C):

E = Adjustment for lost instructional days (lost days × C):

F = Estimated on-task time percentage (typically 50%):

G = Actual instructional/learning time available (D − E x .50[F]):

H = # of objectives to be taught in a given year:

I   = Average time available to teach each objective (G ÷ H):

Note. This form is adapted with permission from the **JOPERD** (*Journal of Physical Education, Recreation & Dance*), August, 1989, p. 32. **JOPERD** is a publication of the American Alliance for Health, Physical Education, Recreation and Dance, 1900 Association Drive, Reston, VA 22091-1599.

Chapter 3

Creating an Atmosphere for Learning

Objectives
As a result of completing the tasks in this chapter you will be able to

- describe major variables that contribute to the development of a positive learning atmosphere;
- understand the important role of teacher expectancy in developing a learning environment;
- develop positive rules for a physical education class; and
- understand the role ownership by the children plays in developing these rules.

WHAT DO YOU EXPECT?

Listed here are many variables important for creating a positive learning environment. Describe your expectations for each variable. What do you realistically expect your students to learn about each variable?

When they enter the gym or playground:

When they hear the stop signal:

When you (or another child) is talking:

When they get out the equipment:

When you are talking and they have equipment:

When they are selecting a partner or group:

When they put equipment away:

When they leave the gym or playground:

We know that successful teachers more than just hope children will behave. They actually expect them to and are willing to spend time creating a learning environment. As you review your expectations, are they just hopes or do you really expect to create an environment in which children work with you to create a positive learning environment?

DECIDING UPON YOUR RULES

Students of successful teachers know the rules that they are expected to follow in P.E. class. Write your rules (maximum of five). Be sure they are positive and easy for students to understand.

1.

2.

3.

4.

5.

VIDEOTAPE ANALYSIS OF A LEARNING ENVIRONMENT

Have someone videotape one of your lessons or another teacher's. Review the tape, then use this form to analyze the learning environment.

Variables	*Comments or Suggestions*
Entering the gym	
Listening to the teacher	
Getting out equipment	
Listening and holding equipment	
Selecting partners	
Response to start signal	
Response to stop signal	
Putting away equipment	
Leaving the gym	

After completing the videotape exercise, what thoughts do you have about the kind of learning environment you or another teacher created with this class?

REFLECTING ON PAST TEACHERS

Over the years you have known teachers who displayed characteristics described in chapter 3—they were firm, but warm and critically demanding. Describe their characteristics and what they did in their classes. Share your descriptions with someone else.

Firm, But Warm:

Critically Demanding:

DEVELOPING A VIDEOTAPE TO TEACH YOUR PROTOCOLS

One suggestion in chapter 3 of the text is to develop a videotape to teach management protocols. Show why the protocols are necessary by asking a class to demonstrate off-task behaviors. Identify four variables and describe the scenes you might include on the videotape to show the wrong way and the right way. How would you help students understand why the protocols are necessary for enjoyable and productive physical education classes?

Protocol	*Wrong Way*	*Right Way*
1.		
2.		

	Protocol	*Wrong Way*	*Right Way*
3.			
4.			

DEVELOPING OWNERSHIP OF THE RULES

It is the beginning of the school year. One of your tasks is to help your students develop ownership of the rules to help them better understand the rules and why they are necessary. As specifically as possible describe how you would do this. Would you do it in the gym? The classroom? On the first day? For all variables? What if one class suggested a different rule than another class? Would you give them the rules and ask them to react? Or would you ask them to suggest the rules? How long would you plan to spend to develop ownership?

Chapter 4

Minimizing Off-Task Behavior and Discipline Problems

Objectives
As a result of completing the tasks in this chapter you will be able to

- describe and analyze strategies to minimize misbehavior;
- compare and contrast Canter's Assertive Discipline Model and Hellison's Levels of Affective Development;
- describe examples of how "assertive communication" might be used in a discipline confrontation; and
- develop strategies describing how a P.E. teacher might work with a classroom teacher, a principal, and parents or guardians to help chronically misbehaving children become more disciplined.

STRATEGIES FOR MINIMIZING MISBEHAVIOR

Chapter 4 of the text suggests strategies that successful teachers use to minimize off-task behavior. Select 10 minutes from a videotape of a children's physical education lesson, preferably a segment somewhat into the lesson rather than in the first few minutes. Using the following form, try to observe each strategy as it is implemented (or when it might have been). Quickly comment for later discussion, about the use of the strategy. If possible, record the exact time on the tape you saw the strategy being implemented. A group can watch and code the same segment and then discuss it after the segment is completed.

Strategies	*Comments*
Back-to-the-wall	
Proximity control	
With-it-ness	
Selective ignoring	
Overlapping	
Use of names	
Positive pinpointing	

Which of the strategies appeared to help minimize or eliminate off-task behavior? Might strategies that weren't used have been helpful? If you observe no off-task behavior in the lesson, it may be because of the way the teacher used some of these strategies.

DISCIPLINE SYSTEMS

Imagine it is the beginning of the school year and you, as the teacher, are explaining your discipline system to the children. Briefly describe six key points you would make to the children if you were explaining Canter's Assertive Discipline System and Hellison's Affective Levels.

Key Points of the Assertive Discipline System

1.

2.

3.

4.

5.

6.

Key Points of the Affective Levels System

1.

2.

3.

4.

5.

6.

Which system do you think you would use (or are you using) in your program? Explain your reasons. Try to discuss your responses with others, remembering that this is not a right/wrong discussion—there are viable reasons a teacher might use each system. Consider, for example, your background as a teacher, the characteristics of the school and students, and the number of days per week you teach the children.

CASE STUDY

A student in your class is continually hitting other children. The child is careful to do it when you are not looking. You know it happens, however, and finally (because you are "with it") you see the child hit another in the back. You call the misbehaving child over and begin to talk with the child. Briefly describe what you would say to that child if you were using

Hellison's Levels of Affective Development:

Canter's Assertive Discipline:

Compare the differences in the message received by the child in each system. Which are you most comfortable with? Why?

PERSONAL CHARACTERISTICS OF EFFECTIVE DISCIPLINE

Several characteristics of successful teachers have been described that relate to minimizing disruptions and off-task behavior: firm, but warm; critical demandingness; the ability to provide clear understandings; and minimizing slippage. Conventional wisdom suggests these characteristics are more common for experienced teachers than for beginners. Do you agree? Explain your answer. How might teachers learn to use these characteristics to benefit them as they teach—whether they are novices or veterans?

DISCIPLINE CONFRONTATIONS

One of the least pleasant aspects of teaching is a discipline confrontation—when a youngster overtly disobeys or challenges you. Though every teacher hopes this never happens, it probably will during the course of a year. One of the best ways to handle a discipline confrontation is to be prepared for it—at least as prepared as possible. Using the guidelines described by Fernandez-Balboa as part of Assertive Communication (p. 52 of the text), describe how you might talk with a child in each of the following scenarios.

Scenario 1. Every time you start to instruct the class, one child interrupts— talking out loud, pushing others nearby, refusing to stay in one place to hear your instructions. After directing the rest of the class to begin a new task, you tell the interruptor to remain to talk with you. Describe your interaction.

Scenario 2. A child who is continually misbehaving is "timed out," but refuses to stay in time-out. When you try to talk with the child, the response is, "There's no way you can make me stay in time-out. This class is a joke!" Describe your interaction.

Scenario 3. One child in your class is older than the other students, has poor skills, and constantly bullies the smaller children. You have tried time-out several times, but it doesn't seem to be effective. What interaction might you have with that child?

If possible, compare your interactions with others. Be aware of various ways a teacher might find to minimize off-task behavior and yet treat children with dignity and respect.

CLASSROOM TEACHERS, THE PRINCIPAL, AND PARENTS

Besides their own ideas, teachers typically have three additional resources to help students who are simply unable to function effectively in a class setting—the student's classroom teacher, the principal, and the parent or guardian. Obviously, each of these persons has a different relationship with a child. Briefly describe how you might ask a classroom teacher, a principal, and a parent or guardian for help with a misbehaving child. Also describe what you would ask that individual to do.

Classroom Teacher:

Principal:

Parent or Guardian:

If possible, compare your responses with others. Discuss how the context of a school might influence your responses.

Chapter 5

Getting the Lesson Started

Objectives
As a result of completing the tasks in this chapter you will be able to

- describe ways a teacher can encourage children to become involved in productive activity as soon as they enter the gym or playground;
- discuss why instant activity may not always be an effective teaching strategy;
- provide examples of set induction for both a lesson and an entire year; and
- critically discuss alternatives to calisthenics and running laps as a way to begin every physical education class.

POSTERS DESCRIBING INTRODUCTORY ACTIVITY

Imagine five rectangles as posters. In each, list one or more activities that you might use to instantly involve your students in physical activity. In at least three, list two or more activities that require students to read the poster rather than just rely on what they see other children doing. Try to design one poster for children who can't read yet.

INSTANT ACTIVITY PROTOCOL

Chapter 3 of the text describes how to develop management protocols to teach children routines that will help their P.E. classes operate smoothly with little wasted time. You need to teach children how to enter a gym (or playground) and begin activity immediately. How might you teach the children to engage in instant activity? Describe how you would teach them to read a poster or description on a chalkboard, for example, or recall instructions from the last lesson so they could start as soon as they reach the physical education class. Assume that students will need several tries to learn this lesson, so prepare several examples. Write the words you would say to the children. If possible, compare your descriptions with others.

VIDEOTAPE ANALYSIS

Try to find three videotapes of physical education lessons (ideally ones that you made before you started to read *Teaching Children Physical Education*). For each lesson, determine how long it was before the majority of the children were involved in activity. What percent of the lesson went by before the children became involved in activity? Comment on the three lesson beginnings from the perspective of a child who is excited about coming to physical education class but has to wait for several minutes before activity commences.

Lesson 1

_____ Number of minutes before majority of children were involved in activity

Comment:

Lesson 2

_____ Number of minutes before majority of children were involved in activity

Comment:

Lesson 3

_____ Number of minutes before majority of children were involved in activity

Comment:

WHEN INSTANT ACTIVITY MIGHT NOT BE EFFECTIVE

As any veteran teacher can tell you, some days instant activity won't be effective or the best way to begin a lesson. Describe three scenarios that illustrate when instant activity may be counterproductive—or even unsafe—for students.

Scenario 1:

Scenario 2:

Scenario 3:

If possible compare and discuss your scenarios with others.

SET INDUCTION

Chapter 5 of the text defines and illustrates set induction or anticipatory set and how they might be used to stimulate children's interest in a lesson. Brief descriptions of five scenarios follow. For each scenario, describe a set induction that might heighten the children's interest in the lesson. Try to make your set inductions creative and contemporary.

Scenario 1. You teach a third-grade class how to pace itself when running a long distance.

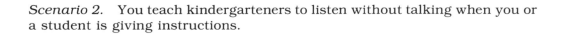

Scenario 2. You teach kindergarteners to listen without talking when you or a student is giving instructions.

Scenario 3. You teach fifth graders how to maintain appropriate spacing (so they don't bunch up) when they play a team game such as soccer or basketball.

Scenario 4. You teach second graders to kick a ball with their insteps rather than with their toes.

Scenario 5. You teach fourth graders to select partners of the opposite gender.

PHYSICAL EDUCATION VOCABULARY BULLETIN BOARD

In the rectangle below, design a bulletin board that gives children the vocabulary (content) of your physical education program. If appropriate, indicate the dates you will study each content area. Try to create a design that will appeal to the children. Be sure to title your bulletin board.

CALISTHENICS AND LAPS AS INTRODUCTORY ACTIVITIES

One way we have traditionally started physical education classes is with calisthenics (often the same ones every day) and then with running laps. Today many P.E. teachers use alternative ways to start class. Based upon your experience and technical knowledge, list several reasons some teachers no longer begin their classes with calisthenics and laps. Compare your reasons with others.

Chapter 6

Instructing and Demonstrating

Objectives
As a result of completing the tasks in this chapter you will be able to

- provide examples of effective instruction and demonstration techniques used when teaching children;
- accurately code the time children spend in a physical education lesson in various activities and interpret the meaning of the time analysis;
- provide examples of checking for understanding and how it can be used to be certain children are comprehending your explanations; and
- discuss the advantages or disadvantages of the technique known as play-teach-play.

BEFORE YOU BEGIN

At the beginning of the textbook I suggest that you make several videotapes of yourself teaching. I hope that by now you've had a chance to do so, because many of the upcoming activities will be far more meaningful if you can analyze your own teaching rather than someone else's. Even if you don't have access to a class of children, just videotape or audiotape several 10- or 15-minute lessons as you teach a friend and you will learn a lot about your tendencies as a teacher.

DISTRACTING HABITS

Have any distracting verbal habits crept into your teaching? Using a videotape or audiotape of yourself teaching, listen for any word or phrase ("ok," "uh," "umm," "you know") that you think you might use regularly and write it down. As you continue the tape, tally how many times you say that word or phrase. This self-check will reveal any distracting habits in your speaking patterns—and simply being aware should go a long way toward eliminating them.

ORGANIZATIONAL AND INFORMATIONAL INSTRUCTING

Find an episode on a videotape or audiotape where you are talking to students, ideally at the beginning of a lesson. Write down verbatim everything you said to the children, and then answer the following questions.

- Was the activity clearly explained (from my verbal instructions, was it possible for the children to know what to do exactly as I had intended)?
- Did I provide too much information (either organizational or descriptive)?
- Did I repeat myself? Was it necessary?
- Did I provide good and clear examples?

The reason I asked you to write down every word you said is to help you reflect on your verbal habits. Actually recording our verbal instructions helps us more clearly understand and evaluate how we talk to children. Although it is time-consuming, it can help you become a more effective teacher.

ANALYZING YOUR INSTRUCTING

Chapter 6 in the text describes four characteristics of effective instruction (pp. 65-68). I have organized these characteristics into a format for analysis. Select three instructional episodes (where you are actually teaching a concept or a skill) from a lesson you have taught and answer the questions related to each guideline. For this exercise, select episodes toward the middle of a lesson rather than your initial instructions to the children.

Instructing Guidelines	Example 1	Example 2	Example 3
Was one idea presented at a time?			
Was the instruction brief?			
Did I use a reminder word or phrase?			
Was my selection of content based on observing the children?			

After analyzing these three instructional episodes what have you learned about your teaching? Your tendencies? Don't be afraid to feel good about yourself, by the way. If you did a great job pat yourself on the back; these exercises are intended both to help you understand how to be a better teacher and to help you realize you already do many things well in your teaching.

DEMONSTRATING

This exercise is much like the previous. In fact, you may want to look at the same three episodes—assuming, of course, that you used a demonstration as part of your instruction. This time, however, analyze your demonstrations using a checklist. (If you are unable to find any demonstrations in your lesson, you may want to think about why you didn't use any.)

Demonstration Guidelines	Example 1	Example 2	Example 3
Was your location correct?			
Whole followed by part demonstration?			
Normal followed by slow demonstration?			
Did you provide a verbal focus?			

Comment on the way you use demonstrations in your teaching. Is there anything you want to change or are you satisfied that your demonstrations are effective?

CHECKING FOR UNDERSTANDING

Select five different skills, concepts, or activities that you enjoy teaching. For each, write two examples of how you might check to be certain students are comprehending your instruction. Try to vary the ways you check (i.e., don't always ask them to raise their hands).

Skills or Concepts	*Ways to Check for Understanding*
1.	
2.	
3.	
4.	
5.	

PLAY-TEACH-PLAY

The play-teach-play technique is explained in Chapter 6 of the text. This technique asks children to play an activity early in a lesson and then practice one or more of the skills before returning to the activity. Suggest three activities that might work effectively for a class of fifth graders more interested in playing than learning. After describing the activity, indicate which skills (or concepts) you might focus on during the teaching phase of the lesson.

Activity Description (Play)	*Skills or Concepts (Teach)*
1.	1.

Activity Description (Play)	*Skills or Concepts (Teach)*
2.	2.
3.	3.

If you are working in a group, compare your activities (and the skills or concepts you would teach that are a part of the activity) with others. Then discuss the pros and cons of the play-teach-play technique and when and how it might be effective and ineffective.

ANALYZING STUDENTS' USE OF TIME

In chapter 6 of the text (pp. 70-72) you will find an explanation of how to use the form on page 38 to determine how children in your classes spend their time. This form is blank. Alone, or with a partner, analyze one (or more) of the lessons on the self-study videotape. Remember, these are consolidated lessons, so the categories may not accurately reflect the actual time children spend in each category.

Students' use of time coding form

Teacher _____ Class _____

Date _____ # of students _____ over 50% of students _____

Time analysis codes: Decision is based on what 51% of the observed students are doing at the time.

M = Management: Time when *most* students (over 50%) are *not* receiving instruction or involved in lesson activity (e.g., changing activities, getting out or putting away equipment, listening to behavior rules or reminder).

A = Activity: Time when most students (over 50%) are involved in physical movement (e.g., catching a ball, throwing at a target, running).

I = Instruction: Time when most students (over 50%) are receiving information about how to move or perform a skill (e.g., how to move using all the space, watching a demonstration, listening to instructions).

W = Waiting: Time when most students (over 50%) are *not* involved in the other categories (e.g., group activity but only one or two are participating, waiting for a turn, off-task behavior, waiting for the teacher to give directions).

```
   1       2       3       4       5       6       7       8       9      10
| | | | | | | | | | | | | | | | | | | | | | | | | | | | | | | | | | | | | | | |

  11      12      13      14      15      16      17      18      19      20
| | | | | | | | | | | | | | | | | | | | | | | | | | | | | | | | | | | | | | | |

  21      22      23      24      25      26      27      28      29      30
| | | | | | | | | | | | | | | | | | | | | | | | | | | | | | | | | | | | | | | |
```

Percent of M time = _____ ÷ _____ = _____ %
                        TOTAL M seconds   TOTAL LESSON seconds

Percent of A time = _____ ÷ _____ = _____ %
                        TOTAL A seconds   TOTAL LESSON seconds

Percent of I time = _____ ÷ _____ = _____ %
                        TOTAL I seconds   TOTAL LESSON seconds

Percent of W time = _____ ÷ _____ = _____ %
                        TOTAL W seconds   TOTAL LESSON seconds

Chapter 7

Motivating Children to Practice

Objectives
As a result of completing the tasks in this chapter you will be able to

- understand how to modify tasks (activities) to make them easier or harder to motivate children by matching the task with ability level;
- describe ways to modify traditional activities to make them more appropriate; and
- design practical examples of techniques that can be used to heighten the motivation of children by using teaching by invitation, intratask variation, child-designed activities, task sheets, and learning centers.

SUCCESS ORIENTED

Chapter 7 of the text shows three ways equipment can be adjusted to make a task easier or harder. One example involves children deciding how far away to place a cardboard box into which they are trying to throw a beanbag. Describe three more throwing skills tasks that would allow children to modify the task to heighten their success or to make it more challenging.

Example 1:

Example 2:

Example 3:

OBSERVING SUCCESS RATE

The form below (Figure 7.1 from the text) provides a way of estimating success rate for children. Use the form to observe two people at play (at a playground, on a videotape, in a physical education class) and code their trials for 10 to 15 minutes. Compute their success ratio and then comment on their success in the context of the setting in which they are being observed. For example, would you expect success rate to be different at recess than during a structured P.E. setting? Would you expect the success rate of adult learners to be different than children's?

Analysis of practice opportunities and success rate

Teacher's name _____ Observer's name_____

Directions: Select one child (try to make it a highly skilled child) and another child (try to make it a low skilled child). Each time they attempt the skill presented in the task (kick with the instep, catch a ball, etc.) mark an "S" if the attempt is successful; mark a "U" if the attempt is unsuccessful. Switch your observation from one child to the other every other minute.

Criterion skill _____

Child #1	*Child #2*
Total successful _____	Total successful _____
Total unsuccessful _____	Total unsuccessful _____
Total attempts _____	Total attempts _____
Success rate (Total successful ÷ Total attempts) _____	Success rate (Total successful ÷ Total attempts) _____

ELIMINATING PUBLIC FAILURE

A spelling bee, in which you're out after one misspelling, is an example of how teachers structure public failure. Unfortunately, P.E. classes in the past also have structured public failure. Here, I list three activities that often cause children to fail publicly. Describe how children might fail publicly under each of the activities. Then provide an "appropriate practice" that will avoid the damage to self-concept that can result, for example, from being eliminated from an activity.

Inappropriate Practice	*Appropriate Practice*
Elimination dodgeball	

Inappropriate Practice	*Appropriate Practice*
Relay races	
Kickball	

TEACHING BY INVITATION

One way to make tasks more developmentally appropriate is to give children opportunities to modify a task so it is easier or harder. Several examples are listed in chapter 7 of the text. Write five tasks that use teaching by invitation (make your five tasks similar to the ones described in chapter 7). Write each task so students feel comfortable choosing either option—try not to make them feel that one option is better than the other.

Example 1:

Example 2:

Example 3:

Example 4:

Example 5:

If you are working in a group, compare your invitations with others. How do you feel about teaching by invitation? When would it be effective? When ineffective?

INTRATASK VARIATION SCENARIO 1

You are teaching a fifth-grade class of 28 children. Your lesson is on kicking. Seven children (five boys and two girls) in the class have been on soccer teams since they were 5 years old; consequently they are excellent kickers. The 21 other students, however, can't kick a moving ball with any degree of accuracy. Describe how you might use intratask variation to design a lesson that is developmentally appropriate for all children in the class.

Kicking Scenario:

INTRATASK VARIATION SCENARIO 2

You are teaching a tumbling lesson—rolling in different directions—to a class of third graders. Most students can't roll backward smoothly. Three children in the class (two girls and one boy) are excellent gymnasts. Describe how you might use intratask variation to allow them to participate in the lesson without becoming bored or off-task.

Tumbling Scenario:

Now that you have described two intratask variation scenarios, reflect on what you might tell (or do with) the children so they'll understand that not everyone will always do the same activity at the same time. In other words, how would you prepare children for intratask variation so that it becomes an effective teaching technique for you?

MODIFYING TASKS TO HEIGHTEN SUCCESS

On a videotape (or in class) observe several children as they play. Watch them perform an activity and determine how it might be made easier or harder to best match their ability levels. Try to observe with a partner so you can compare ideas.

CHILD-DESIGNED ACTIVITIES

One way to motivate children and help make activities more developmentally appropriate is to ask them to design their own game or dance or sequence. Describe how you might do this for fourth graders. Pick a content area you know well and describe what you would say to the children.

Skills (Concepts) to Be Taught:

Equipment:

Number of Children:

Boundaries:

Your Directions to the Children:

Try to compare your directions with someone else's in your group to see how they might instruct the children. If you are working in a group, it is interesting if you all choose the same content area (e.g., kicking games, a sequence that includes jumping and landing, a balance, rolling).

TASK SHEETS

Task sheets are described in chapter 7 of the text as one way to heighten children's success by encouraging them to work at their own pace. An example of a task sheet for striking with paddles is on page 87 of the text. Now, design your own task sheet for a content area with which you are familiar. Be certain that tasks progress logically from easier to harder. Decide how you will ask the children to verify their progress—by the teacher, a classmate, a parent? Provide instructions at the top of the sheet.

Task Sheet for _____

Grade levels:

Directions:

Tasks:

  1.

  2.

  3.

  4.

  5.

  6.

  7.

  8.

  9.

  10.

Do you use (or plan to use) task sheets in your teaching? Why or why not?

STATIONS OR LEARNING CENTERS

Stations, or learning centers, are described in chapter 7 of the text as another way to motivate children to enjoy and benefit from P.E. lessons. Diagram a learning center format with eight stations for a primary-grade class. Assume you have 22 students. Write the directions as you would say them to the children for each station.

Diagram of Learning Centers (Eight Stations)

Directions for Station 1:

Directions for Station 2:

Directions for Station 3:

Directions for Station 4:

Directions for Station 5:

Directions for Station 6:

Directions for Station 7:

Directions for Station 8:

Overall Directions

Stop/start signal:

Direction to rotate:

What to do with the equipment:

Chapter 8

Observing and Analyzing

Objectives
As a result of completing the tasks in this chapter you will be able to

- accurately distinguish between subject- and child-centered teaching; and
- describe techniques effective teachers use to better see what children are (or aren't) learning.

SUBJECT- AND CHILD-CENTERED TEACHING

Chapter 8 of the text provides two examples of subject-centered teaching—a dribbling activity for kindergarten children and an official volleyball game for intermediate-grade children. No doubt you can recall other activities that were inappropriate for the class (i.e., too advanced for most children). Think back on your experiences in physical education and describe below three activities that were obviously too hard—or perhaps too easy—for the class. Briefly describe the activities and indicate why they were too hard or too easy.

Activity 1:

Activity 2:

Activity 3:

Why do you think teachers sometimes provide subject-centered rather than child-centered activities? Is it simply a matter of observation—or is it more than that?

WHICH CUE IS THE RIGHT ONE?

Select one skill or activity you know well that is typically taught to first graders. List another skill you know well that is typically taught to fifth graders. List three cues typically used to help individuals improve their performance of these skills. Rank order the cues (i.e., the ones you think would be most to least helpful).

Skill Typically Taught to First Graders:

Cues:

1.

2.

3.

Skill Typically Taught to Fifth Graders:

Cues:

1.

2.

3.

For both examples, how would you know which cue to emphasize in your teaching? In other words, what would you observe that would tell you which cue to focus on in your instruction and demonstrations?

DIFFERENCES BETWEEN EXPERT AND NOVICE OBSERVATION

You will need a partner for this activity. Advance a videotape to the middle of a lesson. Play the tape for a maximum of 3 seconds. Stop the tape. Both you and a partner should quickly write down as much as you are able to remember of that lesson. What were the children doing? The teacher? What was the focus? Were the children on- or off-task? Was the lesson safe?

If you say 3 seconds isn't very long to make decisions such as these, you're right. As we gain experience, however, we are able to make rapid and often correct observations about what is and what is not going on in a lesson. In fact, this is one of the skills that distinguishes expert from novice teachers. Try to view a tape you haven't seen so you are forced to make some judgments about an unknown lesson. If no videotape is available, select a photo from a book on teaching physical education that depicts children in action. Look at it for 3 seconds or less, then quickly write your observations. When both you and your partner are finished writing, compare what you have observed. Now go back to the tape or book and compare your perceptions.

BACK-TO-THE-WALL

As you teach, how do you move around the playground or gym? Is your back to the wall or are you in the middle a good deal of the time? Diagram your gym (or playground area). Then have an upper-grade student draw on the diagram the path you travel as you teach. When the lesson is completed, record your reactions to the diagram. Would you change anything? Are you satisfied with the travel pattern? In every lesson a teacher will probably spend some time with his or her back turned to some of the children. (If you are not teaching yet, observe an instructor at your college or university. Whenever the instructor stops to interact with a student, make an "X" on the chart to indicate an individual interaction.)

Diagram of Gym/Playground

Comments about teacher's travel:

SCANNING

Experts can quickly summarize and analyze a situation. This is a learned skill derived from experience and practice. You will need a partner for this task. Select a situation to observe—cooks in the cafeteria, an ongoing class, students walking to and from class, an office. Set a time limit of 15 seconds or less to scan the scene. After scanning write down all you can remember that answers the question "What was going on there?" Be specific. When you finish, compare notes with your partner. What did you see differently? The same? Did you disagree on any observations? Pick several other scenarios and describe them as completely as possible. Practicing this technique will help you quickly summarize a situation and enable you to make better, more informed, and more accurate teaching decisions.

KEY OBSERVATION QUESTIONS

I describe key observation questions in the final section of chapter 8 of the text. Use Figure 8.1 to analyze two situations described earlier—the kindergarten dribbling activity and the intermediate-grade volleyball game—as examples of subject-centered teaching. Recreate, as best you can, the situation in your mind from the descriptions provided. Describe what your thoughts might be about each question in each scenario.

Kindergarten Dribbling:

    Safe?

    On-task?

    Change task for entire class?

    Change task for individuals?

Intermediate-Grade Volleyball:

    Safe?

    On-task?

    Change task for entire class?

    Change task for individuals?

    Do you find this diagram helpful? How would you use it when you are teaching?

Chapter 9

Developing the Content

Objectives
As a result of completing the tasks in this chapter you will be able to

- make tasks more or less difficult using the principles described in chapter 9 of the text;
- distinguish between cues useful for working with low and high skilled children;
- develop challenges (applications) that are motivating to children based on the principles described in chapter 9; and
- analyze content development patterns using a provided form.

MAKING TASKS EASIER OR HARDER

Chapter 9 of the text describes ways to make a task easier or harder so children receive maximum benefit. Outline how you could make tasks easier or harder using the principles described in chapter 9. Two beginning tasks are suggested, but feel free to devise your own. As appropriate, modify the tasks as suggested by the explanation of that principle. Every principle will not apply to every task. In a gymnastics or dance setting, for example, the introduction of a defender would not make sense.

Beginning Task Number 1. Throw the ball hard against the wall and try to catch it.

Static   *Dynamic*

Single Movement	Combination Movement

Alone	With a Partner or Group

Equipment	Variation of Equipment

No Defender	Defender

Beginning Task Number 2. Jump and land on two feet.

Static	Dynamic

Single Movement	Combination Movement

Alone	With a Partner or Group

Equipment	Variation of Equipment

No Defender	Defender

BEGINNER AND ADVANCED CUES

Successful teachers provide different cues by gauging their students' abilities. It would not make sense, for example, to focus on kicking the ball with the instep if all students already could. Instead the teacher might choose to focus on how to kick so the ball travels high or low, on the spot where the foot contacts the ball, or on the follow-through. As the ability of the children improves the cues are changed. Select five skills you know well and provide a cue to use with beginners and a cue to use when teaching advanced students.

Skill Number 1:

Beginning Cue   *Advanced Cue*

Skill Number 2:

Beginning Cue   *Advanced Cue*

Skill Number 3:

Beginning Cue   *Advanced Cue*

Skill Number 4:

Beginning Cue   *Advanced Cue*

Skill Number 5:

Beginning Cue   *Advanced Cue*

Be certain you listed cues and not tasks. Sometimes the two are confused. Try to compare your chart with someone else's in your group to see cues they would suggest as beginning and advanced.

CREATING INTERESTING CHALLENGES FOR CHILDREN

Successful teachers find ways to maintain children's interest in practicing tasks so they can improve. One way is by using interesting and creative applications that students find enjoyable and challenging. Following are suggestions for creating challenges or applications as described in chapter 9 of the text. Complete the chart for the two tasks (throwing and jumping) that you worked on earlier. As was true with the section on cues, all principles may not apply to both of the tasks.

Principle	_Task: Throw the ball hard against the wall and try to catch it_	_Task: Jump and land on two feet_
Repetitions		
Timing		
Keeping score		
Replays		
Videotape		
Performing for an audience		
Performing for young children		

Try to compare your responses with several others' in your group. This helps you realize many creative ways to challenge children.

CONTENT DEVELOPMENT PATTERNS

Chapter 9 of the text describes ways P.E. teachers develop lesson content. Use the form on page 55 and analyze the way a teacher develops content by first writing (in abbreviated form) comments related to content development (extensions, refinements, and applications) that are made to the entire class (not individual students). When the lesson is completed, graph the pattern of the content development. There are several ways to complete this task. You may want to

1. analyze the videotape you made earlier of your teaching;
2. observe a teacher (it really doesn't matter what level) and analyze content development; and/or
3. analyze content development in one of the videotaped companion lessons.

Although it may not be practical, try to compare your analysis with someone else. This will allow you to discuss and clarify your analysis. When you observe an actual lesson it will probably not be as straightforward as it appears in the book. For example, many of us provide a task and a refinement as part of one instructional episode.

Teacher's name _____ Observer _____

Class taught _____ Date _____

Lesson focus _____

Directions: Write down the statements the teacher makes to the entire class, not to groups or individuals, about motor skills—not about behavior or management. At times you may need to abbreviate but try to capture the intent of the meaning. When the lesson is over, classify each statement as extending (tasks), refining (cues), or applying (challenges). Then graph the statements in the order in which they occur.

1.

2.

3.

4.

5.

6.

7.

8.

9.

10.

Extend
  (tasks)

Refine
  (cues)

Apply
  (challenges)

    1   2   3   4   5   6   7   8   9   10   11   12   13   14   15   16   17   18   19   20

As a follow-up to this exercise, if you are currently teaching you will find it interesting to tape a new lesson and try to develop a content pattern that would enhance your students' involvement.

Skill: _____   **Grade level:** _____

Extensions (tasks)	Refinements (cues)	Applications (challenges)
1.	1.	1.
2.	2.	2.
3.	3.	3.
4.	4.	4.
5.	5.	5.

Note. Deciding on a skill and grade or approximate class skill level, arrange five extensions (tasks) in a logical progression from easier (1) to harder (5). For each task, list one cue in the second column that will help the children learn that task more quickly and efficiently. In the third column, list one challenge or application that will motivate the children to continue practicing that task.

Chapter 10

Providing Feedback

Objectives
As a result of completing the tasks in this chapter you will be able to

- understand your personal speaking habits and trends when teaching children;
- gain an awareness of the type and frequency of feedback provided to children by physical education teachers; and
- be able to distinguish types of physical education teacher feedback and why some types are preferred over others.

ANALYZING TEACHER FEEDBACK

I would guess that a lot of feedback teachers give is general rather than specific. When it is specific it is often incongruent. Why do you think this might be? What causes us to use this type of feedback as opposed to specific, congruent feedback?

Figure 10.1 (p. 123 of the text) shows one way to analyze the quantity and quality of feedback provided by physical education teachers. The form on page 58 is the same one described in the book. Use it to analyze your use of feedback on the video you made of yourself or to analyze one of the mini-lessons on the companion videotape. If you don't know the names of the children identify them by their clothing and record which children are provided feedback—how often and what types. When you have completed the analysis answer the following questions:

1. Who received the teacher's feedback? Was there an evident pattern (e.g., low skilled more than high skilled; boys more than girls)?
2. What types of feedback were provided? Was there an evident pattern?
3. What would you recommend to the teacher on the videotape (or yourself) about feedback provided in the lesson?

Feedback analysis form

Date _____ Class _____ Grade _____

Topic of lesson _____

Names	General feedback	Specific feedback							
		Behavior			Skill			Congruent	
(May not want to list entire class)	(No specific referent)	+	0	−	+	0	−	Yes	No
1.									
2.									
3.									
4.									
5.									
6.									
7.									
8.									
9.									
10.									
11.									
12.									
13									
14.									
15.									
16.									
17.									
18.									
19.									
20.									
21.									
22.									
23.									
24.									
25.									
26.									
27.									
28.									
29.									
30.									

LOW SKILLED AND UNCONFIDENT

Imagine a youngster who is poorly skilled—and knows it. Consequently he does not feel good about himself in physical education classes. Try to put yourself in his shoes. What might the student think when the teacher gives specific, congruent feedback? How might it feel? What happens if the student gets no feedback—and yet knows he is doing poorly?

DEVELOPING FEEDBACK STATEMENTS FROM THE CUES

In the previous chapter of this study guide you identified beginner and advanced cues related to several skills that you know well. Reread that section, write each cue, and then try to condense it for presentation to children in a simple (brief) version. In the example in the text, the idea of "pushing a ball when dribbling with your finger pads" was condensed to "pads" when the teacher was providing feedback.

	Full Cue	*Condensed for Feedback*

Skill Number 1
Beginner Cue:

Advanced Cue:

Skill Number 2
Beginner Cue:

Advanced Cue:

Skill Number 3
Beginner Cue:

Advanced Cue:

Skill Number 4
Beginner Cue:

Advanced Cue:

Skill Number 5
Beginner Cue:

Advanced Cue:

ONE-ON-ONE FEEDBACK

For this task, try to observe two scenarios.

Scenario 1: Observe a parent teaching a child a motor skill—perhaps at a playground, at a golf driving range, or at an ice-skating rink. Observe for several minutes and then write what the parent said to the child.

Scenario 2: Observe a coach working one-on-one with an athlete—for example, in a gymnastics setting, in tennis, or at a track. Observe the interaction for several minutes and then write what the coach said to the athlete.

Comment on the differences and similarities between the two scenarios. Compare your findings with someone in your group. My hunch, no more than that, is that the parent will overload the child with information but that the coach will focus on one or two aspects of the skill.

It seems that in their feedback statements many P.E. teachers tend to provide children with more information than they can truly comprehend and apply. Why do you think this might be true? What are the implications of providing children with simple rather than complex feedback statements?

NEGATIVE FEEDBACK

Imagine that you are observing a lesson on throwing. The teacher focuses on stepping with the foot opposite the throwing arm. You hear the teacher say to several children, "No. That's not the opposite foot. Remember to step with the foot opposite your throwing hand." How do you think the children receiving that feedback will feel? Should the teacher use negative feedback? Is it ever appropriate?

Chapter 11

Questioning and Problem Solving

Objectives
As a result of completing the tasks in this chapter you will be able to

- describe and provide examples of convergent and divergent questioning as used in physical education settings;
- develop scenarios illustrating both convergent and divergent questioning; and
- explain the advantages and disadvantages of questioning and problem solving and how they relate to your personal teaching background and goals.

DEFINING CONVERGENT AND DIVERGENT QUESTIONING

The two terms that are used in chapter 11 of the text to differentiate between the types of questions a teacher might ask are *convergent* and *divergent.* Define in your own words the two terms and then give examples of each. This will heighten your understanding of the terminology. If possible, compare your responses with someone else in your group.

CONVERGENT QUESTIONING SCENARIO

In the textbook (p. 129), you will find several topics suitable for a lesson employing convergent questioning. On page 133, two examples illustrate questions a teacher might ask. Use those examples to describe how you might develop a convergent questioning scenario. Select one of the problems on page 129, or create your own. The following format will help you create your scenario.

Children's Grade Level:

Brief Description of What You Want the Children to Discover:

Initial Question:

Development of Additional Questions Leading to Solution(s):

Closure Statement:

DIVERGENT QUESTIONING SCENARIO

This task calls for you to create another scenario, this time using divergent questioning. Again the examples on page 133 can suggest what you might write. Problems that lend themselves to solving through divergent questioning are suggested on page 130. Use one of those problems or develop your own.

Children's Grade Level:

Brief Description of the Solutions You Expect From the Children:

Initial Question:

Development of Additional Questions Leading to Alternatives:

Closure Statement:

WHY PROBLEM SOLVING?

I suspect convergent and divergent questioning are not much used in physical education teaching. Imagine that you are speaking to a group of teachers. Briefly outline why you believe these two approaches help children and encourage the teachers to incorporate them into their teaching.

PINPOINTING DIVERGENT EXAMPLES

A suggestion in chapter 11 of the text is that *pinpointing* (defined on pp. 72-73) can be used to help encourage children to discover several solutions to a problem. For each suggested divergent questioning problem (p. 130) provide an example of how you might pinpoint children. Understand that you are trying to encourage children to be different rather than alike.

Let me give you a hint. You will probably want to pinpoint children who are finding different solutions to the same problem at the same time. For example, in the first problem you might pinpoint two children who are traveling in different ways (e.g., "Let's watch Pedro and Gail. Notice how Pedro is using a leapfrog type of jump while Gail is traveling using a low-level cartwheel.").

Traveling in General Space:

Balancing on Floor (Apparatus):

Mounting (Dismounting) Bench, Box, Beam:

Outmaneuvering Opponent in a Game:

Alternative Ways to Shoot a Ball:

Dance or Gymnastic Sequences:

Passing a Ball from Player A to Player B:

Creating a Game:

ADVANTAGES AND DISADVANTAGES OF CONVERGENT QUESTIONING

As with any teaching skill or approach described in the text, there are both reasons they might be used and reasons they might not. Suggest three advantages and three disadvantages for using convergent questioning. If you are already teaching, relate your responses to your school. If you are not yet teaching, relate your responses to the elementary school you attended.

Advantages	*Disadvantages*
1.	1.
2.	2.
3.	3.

ADVANTAGES AND DISADVANTAGES OF DIVERGENT QUESTIONING

Do the same thing you did before, but this time try to think of three advantages and disadvantages related to divergent questioning.

Advantages	Disadvantages
1.	1.
2.	2.
3.	3.

PERSONAL PROBLEM SOLVING

We know that teachers are more likely to teach the way they were taught and to teach what they know best. How do you feel as a teacher or future teacher about convergent and divergent questioning? Does one appeal to you more than another? If so, why? How might you more proficiently use these two techniques?

Chapter 12

Building Positive Feelings

Objectives
As a result of completing the tasks in this chapter you will be able to

- heighten your sensitivity to children and their varying abilities and interests;
- analyze and describe your tendencies as a teacher to pay more attention to one group of children than another; and
- describe strategies and techniques for helping all children—regardless of their abilities, appearances, or interests—to feel welcome in P.E. classes and find success leading to enjoyment of physical activity.

UNDERSTANDING CHILDREN'S FEELINGS

Imagine you are a poorly skilled child in a P.E. class. The teacher has just announced that the class is going to play volleyball—one half of the class against the other half. The losing team has to run three laps; the winning team can shoot baskets. What thoughts are going through your head? How do you feel?

Now imagine you are one of the highly skilled children in that same class. How do you feel? What thoughts are going through your head?

Low skilled child:

High skilled child:

Now imagine you are the teacher. How might you redesign this scenario so that both the high and low skilled children have positive feelings about the activity(ies) you have designed? Describe in detail.

WHO DO TEACHERS TEND TO FAVOR?

Watch a videotape of yourself teaching (or one of the lessons in the self-study videotape). Use the form provided in chapter 10 of the text (Form 10.1, p. 123) and page 58 of this study guide to analyze the children who are getting your feedback (or the videotaped teacher's feedback, in which case you will have to identify the children by their clothing). After 15 minutes tally the results to determine who gets your (or the videotaped teacher's) feedback—and what type they receive. Are there any obvious patterns? Boys or girls? High or low skilled? On- or off-task children? We probably all tend to favor one group of children over another. Which group do you tend to favor? Why do you think this is so?

MINIMIZING SOLO REQUIREMENTS

Many games have a solo component in which one team member is featured at a given time in the game (e.g., a pitcher in baseball, a server in volleyball). Select five popular sports and describe how each might be modified to reduce the pressure that some children feel in a solo situation.

Sport	*Modification*
1.	1.
2.	2.
3.	3.
4.	4.
5.	5.

MISTAKES-OK-HERE ZONE

Chapter 12 of the text describes the concept of a mistakes-OK-here zone. Imagine you are talking to a class of third-grade children. Write how you would describe the mistakes-OK-here zone to them so they feel comfortable participating—without worry of failure or embarrassment.

ALTERNATIVE SCORING SYSTEMS

Earlier you identified five sports and modified them to avoid placing children in solo positions. Now use the same five sports and devise an alternative scoring system (p. 143 of the text) that emphasizes cooperation and harmony rather than winning and losing.

Sport	*Alternative Scoring System*
1.	
2.	
3.	
4.	
5.	

HELPING CHILDREN DESIGN THEIR OWN GAMES

Assume you are urging students to learn how to throw and catch efficiently and effectively. As part of the lesson you want children to design their own game that includes practice in throwing and catching. In words you would use with the children, describe the guidelines you would provide so students could successfully design their own games. It often helps to limit some of the choices the children have to make. Try to share instructions with someone else so you can compare ideas.

SHARING TEST RESULTS

Imagine your school district requires you to give your students fitness tests twice a year. Use the guidelines described in chapter 12 of the text to describe how you would let the children know their results in a nonembarrassing way—and also how you might use the test results to encourage them to improve their fitness. Be realistic and assume you are teaching at least 400 children. Understand that children at different grade levels vary in both abilities and understandings. How would you discourage children from comparing their results with one another?

HELPING CHILDREN SET GOALS

Pick an activity you know well and that lends itself to goal setting for children. Describe how you would help children set their own goals to improve in this activity. Once again, be realistic and remember that you are teaching a large number of children.

ENCOURAGING COOPERATION

As a teacher you work hard to help children work with one another in an encouraging atmosphere. In the lesson you are teaching this day, you hear three of your fifth graders laugh out loud when another child falls during class. One says, ''Hope you had a nice trip!'' Another says, ''He will tell you about it next fall.'' Most children in the class hear these remarks. How would you deal with this situation as a teacher? Describe what you would say to the children about this episode. Try to compare your comments with someone else's.

Chapter 13

DO YOU KEEP TRACK OF WHAT THE CHILDREN HAVE LEARNED?

Assessing Children's Progress

Objectives
As a result of completing the tasks in this chapter you will be able to

- describe and develop techniques for assessing children's progress in a physical education program; and
- explain realistic assessment approaches that reflect the fact that elementary P.E. teachers often teach several hundred children.

PRIORITIZING ASSESSMENT

Chapter 13 of the text describes several ways teachers might assess children's improvement in physical education. Obviously a teacher will not be able to or even want to use all of those ideas. But this task can help you prioritize assessment techniques based on your program goals. List in order five assessment techniques you use (or plan to use). Also indicate when you use (or plan to use) them.

Assessment Technique	*When Used*
1.	
2.	
3.	

Assessment Technique	*When Used*
4.	
5.	

BROAD CATEGORIES OF FITNESS TESTING

Chapter 13 of the text suggests broad categories you can use to assess children's improvement on fitness test items. List five fitness test items you might use and the categories (numerical cut-offs) you might use for each item. Have three to five categories for each test item.

Test Item	*Numerical Categories*
1.	
2.	
3.	
4.	
5.	

Try to share your criteria with others in your group.

OBTAINING HELP WITH TESTING

One way some teachers get help with testing is to ask parents to donate their time. For some teachers, the hardest part is simply to ask for help. This task can help you do that hard part. Write a sample letter to parents requesting their help with testing. Be sure to answer such questions as: How long will it take? What is the purpose of the testing? How will I learn to administer the test? What do I need to wear? Will it be inside or outside? What about lunch?

While parents are a logical source of help, think about other sources of help such as retirees or high school students and design your letter accordingly.

ASSESSING MOTOR SKILLS

Chapter 13 of the text contains a suggestion for assessing critical components (Figure 13.3) for striking with rackets. Obviously this is only one of many skills you might teach during a year. Be realistic and design a system for keeping track of six skills (other than striking with rackets) you might teach during a year—along with the critical components. You may not want to assess every skill in every grade level and you may want to assess only one or two critical components of a skill during a year. Assume you teach your children twice a week for 30 minutes. List the six skills you have selected, three critical components for each skill, and the grade levels in which they might realistically be assessed.

Skill	Critical Components	Grade Level
1.	a.	a.
	b.	b.
	c.	c.
2.	a.	a.
	b.	b.
	c.	c.
3.	a.	a.
	b.	b.
	c.	c.

4. a.   a.

    b.   b.

    c.   c.

5. a.   a.

    b.   b.

    c.   c.

6. a.   a.

    b.   b.

    c.   c.

In some ways that was the easy part. Now describe how you might keep track of the children's progress for each component. Assume you teach 500 children each week. Will you use a computer? Ask the children to keep track of their own progress? Ask for parent help? Recruit classroom teachers to help out? Be as thorough as possible in describing your system and account for time constraints. For example, if you use a computer program to keep track of the information, who will enter the scores and how long will it take?

ASSESSING COGNITIVE UNDERSTANDING

Figures 13.4 and 13.5 in the text provide examples of questions a teacher might use to assess children's cognitive understanding. It's important to write questions that reflect what you emphasize in your program and that are written so students can comprehend them. Using the examples in chapter 13 of the text, develop 10 questions that might be useful to ascertain what intermediate-grade children (third-sixth grades) have learned. Use the format from the examples provided or develop your own. Share your questions with others to be certain they are clear. If possible administer them to a group of children. After the students have completed the test, ask them to evaluate their clarity and ease of understanding. As you remember from your tests and measurements class, it takes a lot of time to develop good test questions.

1.

2.

3.

4.

5.

6.

7.

8.

9.

10.

ASSESSING CHILDREN'S ATTITUDES TOWARD PHYSICAL ACTIVITY

This task is similar to the previous one. Figure 13.7 in the text shows how teachers might assess children's attitudes toward a physical education program and their levels of confidence. Use the same procedure to develop 10 questions that will provide you with useful information about how children rate both your program and their confidence in their own abilities. If possible share your test with others in the group. Also ask children to complete your questions and provide you with feedback about each item.

1.

2.

3.

4.

5.

6.

7.

8.

9.

10.

GRADING

You teach in a school of 500 children. Six times a year, you must give a physical education grade to every child. Your choices are Excellent (E), Satisfactory (S), and Needs Improvement (NI). Your principal wants you to document each grade you assign. In other words, your grades must be based on more than just impressions. Describe how you would assign the grades for each 6-week period. Try to incorporate some of the ideas described in this chapter—but be realistic. Compare your ideas with others in your group.

Chapter 14

Continuing to Develop as a Teacher

Objectives
As a result of completing the tasks in this chapter you will be able to

- demonstrate an awareness of activities that appeal to you and that could cause you to continue to grow and improve as a teacher; and
- describe realistic ways a teacher might continue to learn, improve, and remain enthusiastic about teaching over a 30-year career.

CONSEQUENCES OF BECOMING SATISFIED

What happens when a teacher becomes satisfied with his or her teaching and doesn't change for years? You probably have been taught by one or more teachers who fell into this pattern. What was it like as a student? Did you know this teacher was out of touch? What are your memories of this teacher? Try to recall your memories as specifically as you can, share them with others in your group.

POSSIBILITIES FOR CONTINUING TO DEVELOP

Chapter 14 of the text suggests ways teachers can remain abreast of current ideas and developments in teaching. Of the ones described, which appeal most to you? Why? Based on your response, develop a realistic plan describing specifically what you might do to remain current over the next 6 months, 1 year, 2 years. This is for your own improvement. What might you truly be able to do? Which conference might you attend? What book will you read over the summer? When will it work for you to visit another teacher?

Plan for Improvement

6 Months:

1 Year:

2 Years:

DEVELOPING A SUPPORT GROUP

This is a task just for you. Assume you think a support group would be a good idea. Who would you want to be in that group? When would you meet? Where? How would you keep it from becoming a gripe session that is deflating rather than encouraging? How would you get new ideas presented to your group?

Continuing to Develop as a Teacher 81

OBTAINING SUPPORT TO CONTINUE DEVELOPMENT

It is often difficult to find the time and money to stay current. Write a letter to your principal outlining your plans. Use your 3-year plan to make the case why these opportunities are important if you are to grow as a teacher. If you are the only P.E. teacher in the school, you may need to educate the principal how a P.E. teacher's needs are different from the classroom teacher's. Share your letter with others in your group and compare ideas.

SHARING VIDEOTAPES

One increasingly available opportunity for sharing ideas is through videotapes. Briefly describe five videotapes you would find useful.

Videotapes I Would Find Useful

1.

2.

3.

4.

5.

You probably would want to trade videotapes. What three tapes might you make that other teachers would find worthwhile? None? Don't fall into that trap. Every teacher does some things better than others. What are your strengths as a teacher or future teacher? What would other teachers be interested in if they came to your school?

Videotapes I Could Make

1.

2.

3.

STAGES OF TEACHING

Chapter 14 of the text describes Feiman-Nemser's three stages of teaching. In the final task of this study guide think about where you are as a teacher in her analysis. Are you where you want to be? Are you at another stage that she hasn't included? How might you develop to the next stage? Believe it or not, for this task I won't ask you to write anything. Just ponder the question—preferably on a long walk by yourself, or while sitting on top of a mountain, or while in your garden. Think too about the many children that you have the potential to influence in positive ways throughout your career. And be gentle with yourself. The only time to worry is if you conclude you are a perfect teacher with no need to improve.